From Head to Toe

How a Doll Is Made

Susan Kuklin

Hyperion Books for Children
New York

The author would like to thank the following people and organizations:

The Alexander Doll Company
Ira N. Smith
William A. Birnbaum
Therese Stadelmeier
Daun Fallon
Tito Castro
Bruno De Santis
Greta Schrader
Stuart Schwartz
Bill Randall
Allison Smith
Phil Ottenritter
all the staff and the craftspeople

F.A.O. Schwarz
David Niggli

Beryl Jones–Woodin, Peter Woodin, and their children, Eve, Nora, and Lowell

Marshall Norstein

FIRST EDITION

1 3 5 7 9 10 8 6 4 2

Library of Congress Cataloging–in–Publication Data

Kuklin, Susan. From head to toe: how a doll is made/
Susan Kuklin—1st ed. p.   cm.
Includes index.
1-56282-666-2 (trade).—1-56282-667-0 (library)
1. Alexander Doll Company. 2. Doll making—Juvenile literature.
[1. Doll making. 2. Alexander Doll Company.] I. Title.
TS2301.T7K77 1994
688.7'221'097471—dc20 93-23332 CIP AC

This book is set in 14–point Nofret.

For Bailey, with love

A walk through any toy store shows that dolls come in many shapes, sizes, and colors. They can be cuddly babies to hug and squeeze, or they can be elegant porcelain dolls to collect and admire.

Doll making is a special art that takes planning and love from many people. Different things inspire the making of a doll: music, poetry, books, TV, movies. A doll named Autumn is inspired by one of the four seasons.

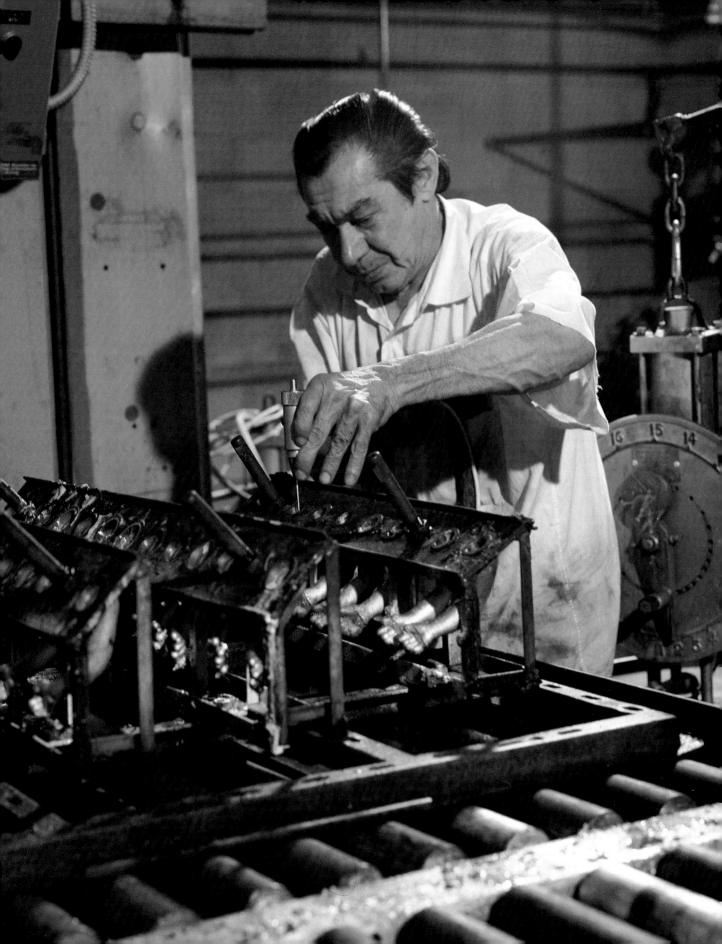

Like most dolls', Autumn's parts begin in a factory. At this particular factory, all the dolls of similar size have the same shape heads and bodies, whether they are male or female, dark- or light-skinned. All the parts are formed in metal molds: head, arms, legs, and body. To make the light-skinned dolls, a worker squirts pink liquid plastic into the molds. They are then sealed and put into an oven. While the plastic bakes, the molds are rotated up and down to make sure the liquid oozes into every part.

A short time later the molds are taken out and dunked into a vat of cold water to cool them enough to handle. After the molds are unsealed, arms, legs, heads, and bodies are pulled out.

Because the parts are still hot, they bend like rubber. It seems that this hot plastic has a memory, because even in later stages when it is reheated and pushed and pulled it cools back to its original shape.

Just as there are people who decide how houses are built, there are people who decide how dolls will look. They are called designers. Daun and Therese are the designers at the factory where Autumn is made. They create different doll characters by choosing clothing, hairstyles, makeup, and skin color.

When they are asked to design four dolls that children could dress up, they both like the idea of a doll for each season. Therese chooses the dolls named for autumn and summer, and Daun chooses dolls modeled after winter and spring.

First the designers talk about the way they think the dolls should look. They also search through books of material, searching for the colors and patterns that will be special for each doll.

Therese says, "After we talk, I think about what the season means to me. I think about the colors of autumn: green, rust, and plum. Then I start sketching."

Daun and Therese fill in the outlines of their sketches with different clothing, hair, and makeup designs. They keep some sketches and reject others. The final choices in the sketches become finished drawings. These drawings are directions to the makeup department, hairstylists, pattern cutters, and dressmakers.

The first finished dolls made from the drawings are called samples. The doll makers make three for the bosses and three for people who will sell the doll to the toy stores. The samples are like a coming attraction for a movie.

Before the parts can be put together, the faces for all the samples have to be designed. Therese says, "I think that Autumn should have really rosy cheeks, bright red lips, and brown eyebrows. I usually test colors and shapes on older, damaged dolls."

Metal stencils are made in order to paint Autumn's lips and eyebrows. A makeup artist follows Therese's directions carefully. She holds Autumn's head behind the stencil, leaving the mouth exposed. Then she sprays red paint onto the mouth area.

Cheeks are sprayed without a stencil. If the makeup artist used one, the doll would have two big solid dots for cheeks and end up looking like a clown. Without a stencil the doll's cheeks get a rosy hue that fades out at the edges.

Therese also chooses the eye color, but the eyes are made separately.

WHOOOOOSH, KABOB, PLUNK! WHOOOOOSH, KABOB, PLUNK! A big brown eyeball attached to an eye–setting machine plunges deep down into Autumn's socket. "You see, baby, that didn't hurt," jokes Wellington, the worker who puts the parts together. Once the eyes, which open and close, are firmly in place, he adjusts them with a screwdriver so that they are even and look straight out. Wellington says, "All the time I'm making a doll I look at her and say, 'How ya doing?' To me, this is a little baby."

Now the heads are ready.

Autumn's body parts are very stiff. Wellington has to make them soft in order to put them together. He places each part under hot orange lights. Then he dips the warmed legs and arms into talcum powder to make them slide easily into their slots.

Now the bodies are ready.

Another doll maker gently pushes the head onto the body. Once Autumn is whole, she is all set for a trip to the hairdressing department.

Raphaela is one of the hairdressers. She fits, cuts, and curls the hair according to Therese's designs. Some dolls have wigs that are glued on, while others have hair rooted directly into their scalps. Therese thought that Autumn would look prettier with a glued wig. She chose a soft, fluffy, hairstyle for Autumn and gave a sample to Raphaela.

Raphaela glues a newly cut wig onto Autumn's head. She styles the hair according to Therese's design, just like a beautician does in the beauty parlor.

Therese says, "Isn't it weird that all my dolls have bushy curly hair just like mine, and Daun's dolls have smooth, straight hair just like hers?"

While Therese plans Autumn's fluffy hair, Daun picks neat and tidy dark brown braids for Winter. Daun chooses to have the doll's hair rooted into her scalp. This is done before the head is attached to the body.

To root hair, another hairdresser uses a special sewing machine threaded with dark brown hair. The hair comes out wild, bushy, long, and ready for styling. After Winter's head is attached to her body, the hairdresser combs and braids it.

Ringlets and curls, flips and bangs—the hairdressers get to work on all kinds of hairstyles.

While the dolls' bodies are being finished, the material cutters work from the patterns that Therese designed. Smaller patterns, for such pieces as a sleeve or a collar, are punched out using metal shapes that look like cookie cutters.

Identical pieces are bundled up and sent to the shoemaking department and to the sewing department, where they are stitched together.

Adelaida, Mercedes, and Kenia work in the sewing department. To make Autumn's clothing, they use nude dolls and Therese's drawing. They work with any fourteen-inch doll because all the doll bodies at the factory are identical.

Each garment has to be carefully measured, from the bow on Autumn's hat right down to the length of her stockings. If the dressmakers see that something is not working in the designer's pattern, they suggest changes. Adelaida says, "The designers leave a lot of space for our creativity. It's a happy process."

Celeste is a dressmaker who works on the details. She sews the delicate lace ruffle on Autumn's extra socks.

The shoemaker, Gomez, puts the doll's shoes together. He sews the tops of the shoes and one by one wraps them around a metal mold. Then he attaches the bottom of each shoe to the top with steamed glue. It's like making a sandwich—only it's a footwich.

W hen the six samples of Autumn are fin–
ished, Therese checks to see that the
clothing, the makeup, and the hairstyle
satisfy her plan. Does the color of the lips go with the
color of her bow? Is the skirt the right length for her
body?

Daun checks, too, since the designers always review each other's work. Daun says, "I don't think we ever loved something that the other one hated. For this project we work especially closely because all four of the dolls' designs must complement one another."

The samples of the Four Seasons are then presented to the designers' bosses, Ira and Bill. Now that they are satisfied with Daun's and Therese's designs, they arrange for many, many more dolls to be made.

nce the actual dolls are made, the final touches are Greta's job. She is the dolls' dresser. She checks to make sure that Autumn's outfits go on and come off easily and that all her parts move perfectly. She carries sharp scissors in case there are any loose threads on the dolls. "I talk to the dolls. I say, 'Look at Mommy. Look at me.' Dolls are great because they smile back—they don't talk back."

Many years ago another dresser taught Greta to make bows. All the material, including the knot, must face right side up. "Look at that bow!" Greta proudly declares when Daun and Therese stop by to see their finished dolls. "How do you like that? I think Autumn looks great. I think she's thrilling." Greta's opinion is important to the designers.

From the factory, hundreds of the Four Seasons dolls are shipped to toy stores all over the world. At a toy store, Nora, Eve, Lowell, and their parents visit the doll department. Lowell holds Autumn and shouts, "Oh, what a beautiful doll!"

When Therese sees her dolls in the arms of children, she says, "This is why we do what we do. We're so happy when we see children having as much fun playing with our dolls as we had creating them."

All the people who helped to make Autumn are proud of their work. They hope they help give children very special friends to play with and love.

DATE			